Popular
PERSIANS

FURRY! GENTLE! DEVOTED!

LOVING! SWEET! SENSITIVE!

ABDO
Publishing Company

Pam Scheunemann

Consulting Editor, Diane Craig, M.A./Reading Specialist

Published by ABDO Publishing Company
8000 West 78th Street, Edina, Minnesota 55439.

Printed in the United States.

 PRINTED ON RECYCLED PAPER

Editor: Liz Salzmann
Content Developer: Nancy Tuminelly
Cover and Interior Design and Production:
   Anders Hanson, Mighty Media
Illustrations: Bob Doucet
Photo Credits: ©Chanan 2009 (pp. 6–7), Shutterstock

Library of Congress Cataloging-in-Publication Data
Scheunemann, Pam, 1955-
 Popular persians / Pam Scheunemann ; illustrations by Bob
Doucet.
    p. cm. -- (Cat craze)
  ISBN 978-1-60453-724-6
  1. Persian cat--Juvenile literature. I. Doucet, Bob, ill. II.
Title.
  SF449.P4S34 2010
  636.8'3--dc22
                          2009005555

Super SandCastle™ books are created by a team of
professional educators, reading specialists, and content
developers around five essential components—phonemic
awareness, phonics, vocabulary, text comprehension, and
fluency—to assist young readers as they develop reading
skills and strategies and increase their general
knowledge. All books are written, reviewed, and leveled
for guided reading, early reading intervention, and
Accelerated Reader® programs for use in shared, guided,
and independent reading and writing activities to support
a balanced approach to literacy instruction.

CONTENTS

The
PERSIAN

A good family cat, a Persian gets used to new places easily. Of all the cat **breeds**, Persians are the most calm. Persians are known for their beauty and loving nature. The Persian is the most popular cat breed in the United States.

FACIAL FEATURES

Head

The head of the Persian cat is large and round. In a side view, the forehead, nose, and chin all line up.

Muzzle

A Persian cat's **muzzle** is very short.

Eyes

The eyes of the Persian are large and round. They are set far apart. The eye color is very bright.

Ears

Persians have small ears with round tips. The ears angle forward and are set low on the head.

4

BODY BASICS

Size
Adult Persians weigh about 7 to 12 pounds (3 to 5 kg).

Build
The Persian is a medium to large cat. It has a broad chest and sturdy body.

Tail
A Persian's tail is short compared to its body length. It does not curve and hangs below the back.

Legs and Feet
A Persian cat's legs are short, thick, and strong. Its paws are large and round.

COAT & COLOR

Persian Fur

The Persian is prized for its long, thick, shiny coat. The thickness comes from having a long topcoat over a long undercoat. Persians have tufts of fur on their ears and toes.

WHITE FUR

BLACK FUR

SOLID BLUE

SHADED SILVER

BLUE SMOKE

Persians come in many different colors and patterns.
The photos on these pages show just a few examples.

BLUE FUR

CREAM FUR

RED FUR

SILVER CLASSIC TABBY

TORTOISESHELL

RED AND WHITE BICOLOR

HEALTH & CARE

Life Span

Persian cats can live for more than 15 years.

Health Problems

A Persian cat's eyes can produce a lot of tears. These tears can stain the fur around the cat's eyes. **Excess** tears should be wiped away with a tissue every day.

8

VET'S CHECKLIST

- Have your Persian spayed or neutered. This will prevent unwanted kittens.

- Visit a vet for regular checkups.

- Avoid exposing your Persian to very hot temperatures.

- Clean your Persian's teeth and ears once a week.

- Clean your Persian's eyes once a day.

- Ask your vet about shots that may benefit your cat.

ATTITUDE & BEHAVIOR

Personality

Persian cats are friendly and gentle. They like to **cuddle** with their owners.

Activity Level

Persians are **relaxed**. They like to sit still instead of playing or running around. They would rather lie in a sunny spot than jump or climb on things.

All About Me

Hi! My name is Pookie. I'm a Persian. I just wanted to let you know a few things about me. I made some lists below of things I like and dislike. Check them out!

Things I Like

- Being around my family
- Stretching out on the couch
- Cuddling
- A regular routine
- Being petted
- A quiet house
- Playing with my toys

Things I Dislike

- Climbing or jumping on furniture
- Loud noises
- Having tangled fur
- Being too hot
- Having teary eyes

LITTERS & KITTENS

Litter Size

Female Persians usually give birth to three to five kittens.

Diet

Newborn kittens drink their mother's milk. They can begin to eat kitten food when they are about six to eight weeks old. Kitten food is different from cat food. It has extra **protein**, fat, and **vitamins** that help kittens grow.

Growth

Persians are born with their eyes closed. Their eyes open when they are two weeks old. Their sight improves slowly. They can't see perfectly until they are about two months old. Persian kittens first stand up when they are two to three weeks old. They should not leave their mother until they are 12 weeks old.

BUYING A PERSIAN

Choosing a Breeder

It's best to buy a kitten from a **breeder**, not a pet store. When you visit a cat breeder, ask to see the mother and father of the kittens. Make sure the parents are healthy, friendly, and well behaved.

Picking a Kitten

Look for a kitten that is friendly. The kitten should be curious and not too nervous. The kitten should be clean and healthy.

Is It the Right Cat for You?

Buying a cat is a big decision. You'll want to make sure your new pet suits your lifestyle.

Get out a piece of paper. Draw a line down the middle.

Read the statements listed here. Each time you agree with a statement from the left column, make a mark on the left side of your paper. When you agree with a statement from the right column, make a mark on the right side of your paper.

I like to cuddle with my cat.	☐	☐	I want an independent cat.
I want a gentle, relaxed cat.	☐	☐	I want an active cat that likes to jump and climb.
I enjoy combing and grooming my cat.	☐	☐	I don't like combing my cat.
I want an indoor cat.	☐	☐	I want to let my cat outdoors.
I don't mind if my cat sheds a lot.	☐	☐	I like a cat that doesn't shed.

If you made more marks on the left side than on the right side, a Persian may be the right cat for you! If you made more marks on the right side of your paper, you might want to consider another breed.

Some Things You'll Need

Cats go to the bathroom in a **litter box**. It should be kept in a quiet place. Most cats learn to use their litter box all by themselves. You just have to show them where it is! The dirty **litter** should be scooped out every day. The litter should be changed completely every week.

Your cat's **food and water dishes** should be wide and shallow. This helps your cat keep its whiskers clean. The dishes should be in a different area than the litter box. Cats do not like to eat and go to the bathroom in the same area.

Cats love to scratch! **Scratching posts** help keep cats from scratching the furniture. The scratching post should be taller than your cat. It should have a wide, heavy base so it won't tip over.

Cats are natural predators. Without small animals to hunt, cats may become bored and unhappy. **Cat toys** can satisfy your cat's need to chase and capture. They will help keep your cat entertained and happy.

Cats should not play with balls of yarn or string. If they accidentally eat the yarn, they could get sick.

Cat claws should be trimmed regularly with special cat claw **clippers**. Regular nail clippers will also work. Some people choose to have their cat's claws removed by a vet. But most vets and animal rights groups think declawing is cruel.

You should comb your cat regularly with a **cat hair comb**. This will help keep its coat healthy and clean.

A **cat bed** will give your cat a safe, comfortable place to sleep.

LIVING WITH A PERSIAN

Being a Good Companion

Although Persians can be large, they are also gentle. They usually get along with other cats and dogs. Persians like attention, but they don't **demand** it.

Inside or Outside?

Persians have such long fur that it must be combed every day. Because of their fur, it is not a good idea to let them outside. Many vets and **breeders** say that it is safest to keep cats inside. That way they are **protected** from predators and car traffic.

18

Feeding Your Persian

Persians may be fed regular cat food. Talk with your vet about choosing the best food for your cat.

Cleaning the Litter Box

Like all cats, Persians are tidy. They don't like smelly or dirty litter boxes. If the litter box is dirty, they may go to the bathroom somewhere else. Ask your vet for advice if your cat isn't using its box.

DANGER:
POISONOUS FOODS

Some people like to feed their cats table scraps. Here are some human foods that can make cats sick.

TOMATOES

POTATOES

ONIONS

GARLIC

CHOCOLATE

GRAPES

THE ROYAL PERSIAN

Longhaired cats probably came from the cold mountain areas of Persia. Persia is now called Iran.

Travelers brought Persian cats to Europe in the 1600s. In Europe, Persian cats were rare and valuable. They were usually the property of royalty. Queen Victoria of England had two Persians.

In 1871, Persian cats were part of the first modern cat show. The show was held at London's famous Crystal Palace. In the late 1800s, Persians were brought to America. They quickly became America's most popular cats. Their beauty and **relaxed** nature make them seem like royalty!

FIND THE PERSIAN

A

B

C

D

THE PERSIAN QUIZ

1. Persians are calm. **True or false?**

2. A Persian's muzzle is very short. **True or false?**

3. A Persian's tail is long compared to its body length. **True or false?**

4. A Persian's eyes should be cleaned once a year. **True or false?**

5. A Persian kitten's eyesight improves slowly. **True or false?**

6. It is safest to keep Persian cats inside. **True or false?**

Answers: 1) true 2) true 3) false 4) false 5) true 6) true

GLOSSARY

breed - group of animals or plants with common ancestors. A *breeder* is someone whose job is to breed certain animals or plants.

cuddle - to hug or hold close.

demand - to require or order someone to do something.

excess - more than the amount desired.

muzzle - an animal's nose and jaws.

protect - to guard someone or something from harm or danger.

protein - a substance found in all plant and animal cells.

relax - to be at rest or at ease.

vitamin - a substance needed for good health, found naturally in plants and meats.

About SUPER SANDCASTLE™

Bigger Books for Emerging Readers
Grades K–4

Created for library, classroom, and at-home use, Super SandCastle™ books support and engage young readers as they develop and build literacy skills and will increase their general knowledge about the world around them. Super SandCastle™ books are part of SandCastle™, the leading preK–3 imprint for emerging and beginning readers. Super SandCastle™ features a larger trim size for more reading fun.

Let Us Know

Super SandCastle™ would like to hear your stories about reading this book. What was your favorite page? Was there something hard that you needed help with? Share the ups and downs of learning to read. We want to hear from you! Send us an e-mail.

sandcastle@abdopublishing.com

Contact us for a complete list of SandCastle™, Super SandCastle™, and other nonfiction and fiction titles from ABDO Publishing Company.

www.abdopublishing.com • 8000 West 78th Street
Edina, MN 55439 • 800-800-1312 • 952-831-1632 fax